DOCUMENTING THE
WAR OF 1812

LEGACY OF THE WAR OF 1812

Lizann Flatt

Crabtree Publishing Company

www.crabtreebooks.com

DOCUMENTING THE WAR OF 1812

Author: Lizann Flatt
Editor-in-Chief: Lionel Bender
Editor: Simon Adams
**Publishing plan research
and development:**
   Sean Charlebois, Reagan Miller
   Crabtree Publishing Company
Proofreader: Crystal Sikkens
Editorial director: Kathy Middleton
Photo research: Bridget Heos
Designer and Makeup: Ben White
**Production coordinator
   and Prepress technician:**
   Margaret Amy Salter
Production: Kim Richardson
Consultant: Richard Jensen,
   Research Professor of History,
   Culver Stockton College,
   Missouri

   Ronald J. Dale,
   War of 1812 Historian,
   1812 Bicentennial Project Manager,
   Parks Canada

Photographic credits:
Alamy: 11t (World History Archive), 25r (Cosmo Condina North
   America), 35 (nagelestock.com), 36 (Jeff Greenberg), 38l (Classic
   Image), 39 (Andre Jenny), 40 (Alliance Images)
Library of Congress: 4 (LC-USZC4-9904), 9r (LC-USZC4-3675), 10 (LC-
   USZ62-2775), 16t (LC-D4-22787), 18t (LC-DIG-ds-00032a), 20 (LC-
   DIG-ppmsca-09855), 25l (LC-D4-4098), 26l (LC-USZC4-3255), 26r
   (LC-USZC4-509), 29b (LC-DIG-ppmsc-02512), 32 (LC-USZ62-
   55883), 33 (LC-DIG-ppmsca-04324), 34 (LC-DIG-ppmsca-18108), 38r
   (LC-USZC2-1969)
shutterstock.com: 1 (Vacclav), 3 (Wally Stemberger), 5 (J.T. Lewis), 16b
   (Jeffrey M Frank), 18m (Wally Stemberger), 23 (J.T. Lewis), 24
   (Adam Berent), 39 (Norman Pogson)
Topfoto (The Granger Collection): 9l, 11b, 12, 13, 14, 15, 17, 19, 21,
   26–27, 28, 29t, 30, 30–31, 36–37
Wikimedia Commons: National Archives of Canada: cover

Maps: Stefan Chabluk

Cover: An oil on canvas painted by Forestier captures the moment on
   December 24, 1814, when British and U.S. diplomats signed the
   Treaty of Ghent in Belgium.
Title page: Today, a statue of Andrew Jackson on a rearing horse
   stands in front of the White House in Washington, D.C.

Library and Archives Canada Cataloguing in Publication

Flatt, Lizann
   The legacy of the War of 1812 / Lizann Flatt.

(Documenting the War of 1812)
Includes bibliographical references and index.
Issued also in electronic format.
ISBN 978-0-7787-7961-2 (bound).--ISBN 978-0-7787-7966-7 (pbk.)

   1. United States--History--War of 1812--Influence--Juvenile
literature. 2. Canada--History--War of 1812--Influence--Juvenile
literature. I. Title. II. Series: Documenting the War of 1812

E357.9.F53 2011   j973.5'2   C2011-905247-4

Library of Congress Cataloging-in-Publication Data

Flatt, Lizann.
   The legacy of the War of 1812 / by Lizann Flat.
      p. cm. -- (Documenting the War of 1812)
   Includes bibliographical references and index.
   ISBN 978-0-7787-7961-2 (reinforced library binding : alk. paper) --
ISBN 978-0-7787-7966-7 (pbk. : alk. paper) -- ISBN 978-1-4271-8830-4
(electronic pdf) -- ISBN 978-1-4271-9733-7 (electronic html)
   1. United States--History--War of 1812--Influence--Juvenile
literature. 2. United States--History--War of 1812--Sources. I. Title.
II. Series.

   E354.F59 2011
   973.5'2--dc23
                                          2011029841

Crabtree Publishing Company

www.crabtreebooks.com   1-800-387-7650

Printed in Canada/082011/MA20110714

Published in Canada
Crabtree Publishing
616 Welland Ave.
St. Catharines, Ontario
L2M 5V6

Published in the United States
Crabtree Publishing
PMB 59051
350 Fifth Avenue, 59th Floor
New York, New York 10118

Published in the United Kingdom
Crabtree Publishing
Maritime House
Basin Road North, Hove
BN41 1WR

Published in Australia
Crabtree Publishing
3 Charles Street
Coburg North
VIC, 3058

CONTENTS

This book includes images of, and excerpts and quotes from, documents of the War of 1812. The documents range from letters, posters, and official papers to battle plans, paintings, and cartoons.

INTRODUCTION

Between 1775 and 1783, the United States had gone through the Revolutionary War and won its independence from Great Britain. Then, in 1812, it decided to go to war once again with Great Britain. This was for several reasons.

Trade, impressment, and land

Great Britain was at war in Europe with Emperor Napoleon of France. As part of the conflict, the British Navy was blocking ports in Europe and later it set up a blockade along the East Coast of the United States. This was to prevent supplies from reaching Napoleon and his allies. This hurt the U.S. economy by preventing trade with Europe.

The United States was also angered because British Navy ships were stopping U.S. ships at sea and forcing anyone it felt to be a British deserter into service in its navy.

Finally, American settlers wanted lands to the west of the Mississippi River. This brought them into conflict with the Native people living there. The settlers suspected that the British, who were allies of the Native people, were helping them fight.

The shape of the war

The United States declared war on Great Britain on June 18, 1812, despite opposition from almost all of the states in New England. The easiest and closest way to strike out at Great Britain was to launch an attack against its lands to the north of the United States in Canada. This is how the war began, but later the conflict spread eastward and southward.

The War of 1812 was fought in three main areas: in and around the Great Lakes and the western territories; in the Atlantic Ocean from Nova Scotia to the West Indies; and in the southern United States. Battles were won and lost on both sides and both sides wanted to end the war.

Above: Colonial leaders Thomas Jefferson, Benjamin Franklin, and John Adams draft the Declaration of Independence from Great Britain in 1776.

The Situation in Canada

In 1812, what is now Canada was part of British North America. It was made up of the colonies of Upper Canada, Lower Canada, Newfoundland, New Brunswick, Nova Scotia, Cape Breton, and Prince Edward Island. Upper Canada was settled in part by Loyalists—Americans who had chosen to remain loyal to Great Britain during the American Revolutionary War. Lower Canada had a large number of French descendants.

In the peace treaty of Ghent, Great Britain and the United States agreed to return to the situation before the war and to settle other differences later.

Conflicts continued

While the war itself ended after three years, on February 18, 1815, the other differences, such as boundary lines, fishing rights, and control of the Great Lakes, took years to settle.

No one really won the War of 1812, and Native North Americans lost much land and their way of life. The situation for African-American slaves

Below: British soldiers in their red uniforms prepare to fire on the Americans in a modern-day reenactment of a battle from the War of 1812.

remained the same in the United States, although some did escape to freedom under British rule. The war helped to shape American and Canadian views of themselves as nations and molded the shape of North America as it is today.

Remembering the war

Today, there are many reminders of the War of 1812. Several present-day places have memorials, commemorations, and reenactments of the battles. In the United States, these include New Orleans, Louisiana; Sackets Harbor, New York; and Baltimore, Maryland. In Canada, there are historic sites at such places as Toronto, Ontario; Allan's Corners, Quebec; and Niagara-on-the-Lake, Ontario.

Right: This map shows the location of major battles in the war.

Below: This map of North America shows country, territory, state, and land claim boundaries as they were at the start of the war.

Land claimed by:
- Great Britain
- Spain
- United States
- U.S. Territories
- Russia

500 kilometers

500 miles

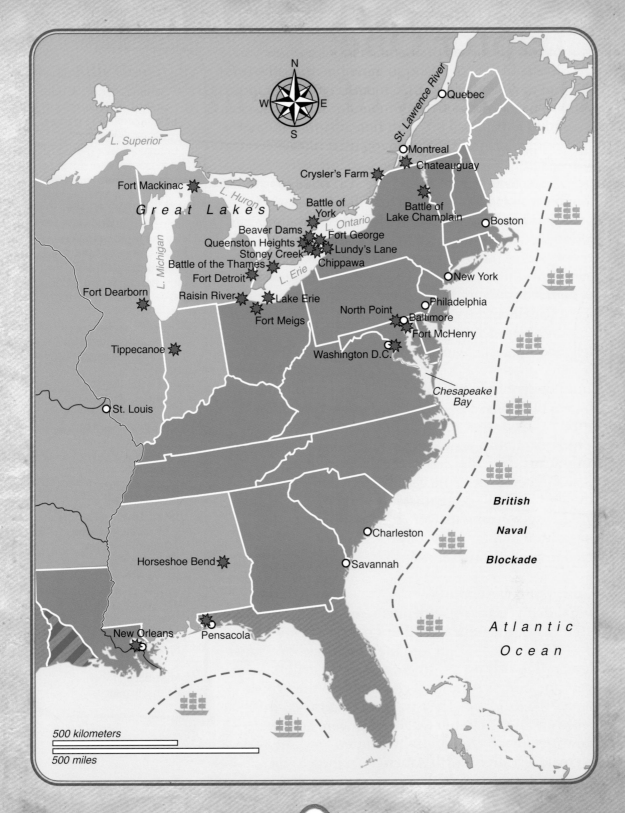

Quebec

St. Lawrence River

Montreal

Chateauguay

Crysler's Farm

L. Superior

Fort Mackinac

Great Lakes

L. Huron

Battle of
Lake Champlain

Boston

Battle of
York

L. Ontario

Beaver Dams
Queenston Heights
Stoney Creek
Battle of the Thames
Fort Detroit

Fort George

Lundy's Lane

Chippawa

New York

Fort Dearborn

Raisin River

L. Erie

Lake Erie

Fort Meigs

North Point

Philadelphia

Baltimore

Fort McHenry

L. Michigan

Tippecanoe

Washington D.C.

*Chesapeake
Bay*

St. Louis

British

Naval

Blockade

Charleston

Horseshoe Bend

Savannah

New Orleans

Pensacola

*Atlantic
Ocean*

500 kilometers

500 miles

Chapter One:
The Treaty of Ghent

The written agreement to end the War of 1812 between Great Britain and the United States is known as the Treaty of Ghent. It took several months before the two sides could agree on the terms of the treaty. Battles had been won and lost on both sides and it was difficult to say who was winning.

Both sides wanted to end the war. In Europe, Great Britain and its allies had been fighting Emperor Napoleon of France and had finally defeated him. The Americans were worried that after British troops were done fighting in Europe, they could be sent to North America. These additional forces could possibly defeat the United States. The British agreed to peace talks because they felt they could negotiate a peace settlement in their favor. Americans were divided in the support of the war, as some members of the government and the New England states were against it. Both the British and U.S. governments were having trouble with opposition in their own countries to raising taxes to continue fighting the war.

Conflicting viewpoints

Initial demands for a settlement were different from what was ultimately agreed upon in the treaty.

The Americans went into the peace talks no longer demanding that impressments—forcing sailors, who were sometimes American citizens, into the British Navy—be dropped. They were willing to accept peace and return to the way things were before the war. Great Britain initially wanted land set aside to create a Native North American nation to the south and west of Lake Erie.

Peace Delegates

Formal negotiations to end the war began in August 1814, in Ghent, in present-day Belgium. The men sent to negotiate the peace settlement were:

British delegates
- James Lord Gambier, Vice-Admiral of the Royal Navy
- Henry Goulburn, a member of the British parliament and Under-Secretary of State for War and the Colonies
- Dr. William Adams, a doctor of maritime and naval law

United States delegates
- John Quincy Adams, a Republican from Massachusetts
- James A. Bayard, a Federalist from Delaware
- Henry Clay, a Kentucky "War Hawk"
- Jonathan Russell, a Rhode Island "War Hawk"
- Albert Gallatin, a Republican from Pennsylvania

They also wanted the boundary between the United States and British North America to change, so that they would control parts of what are now Maine and Minnesota. Great Britain controlled some of these lands at this time with help from the Native people. It wanted to end U.S. rights to fish off the east coast of British North America. Great Britain also wanted the Americans to remove their warships and naval bases from the Great Lakes.

Right: The signing of the peace treaty in Ghent was welcomed by the *Portsmouth Oracle* in New Hampshire in February 1815.

Below: A watercolor painting of late-December 1814, shows a representation of the Treaty of Ghent. Britannia (right) and America (left) hold olive branches as symbols of peace and sailors support their national flags.

PEACE !

Treaty of PEACE signed & arrived !

CENTINEL-OFFICE, *Feb.* 13, 8 *o'cloch in the morning.*

WE have this instant received in Thirty-two hours from N. York, the following

Great and Happy News !

To BENJAMIN RUSSELL, *Esq. Centinel-Office, Boston,*
New-York, Feb. 11, 1815.—*Saturday Evening,* 10 *o'clock.*

SIR—

I HASTEN to acquaint you, for the information of the Public, of the arrival here this afternoon of H. Br. Majesty's Sloop of War FAVORITE, in which has come passenger Mr. CARROLL, American Messenger, having in his possession a

TREATY OF PEACE

Between this Country and Great-Britain, signed on the 26th December last.

Mr. BAKER also is on board, as Agent for the British Government, the same who was formerly Charge de Affairs here.

Mr. Carroll reached town at eight o'clock this evening. He shewed to a friend of mine who is acquainted with him, the pacquet containing the Treaty, and a London Newspaper of the last date of December, announcing the signing of the *Treaty.*

It depends, however, as my friend observed, upon the act of the President to suspend hostilities on this side.

The gentlemen left London the 2d Jan. The *Transit* had sailed previously from a port on the Continent.

This city is in a perfect uproar of joy, shouts, illuminations, &c. &c.

I have undertaken to send you this by Express—the rider engaging to deliver it by Eight o'clock on Monday morning. The expense will be 225 dollars—If you can collect so much to indemnify me I will thank you so to do.

I am with respect, Sir, your obedient servant,

JONATHAN GOODHUE.

Printed at the Portsmouth Oracle-Office.

A turning point arises

The American delegation was surprised by the British demand for a Native North American territory. They did not present the demand to their government. Some Americans in the delegation felt that Great Britain did not want peace and was going to launch a big attack. Both parties thought that peace negotiations would be broken off. The groups went back and forth, rewriting their demands.

Things began to change when Great Britain might need to keep more of its navy in Europe than originally planned. This was the result of a threat of serious disagreement between Great Britain and Russia during talks following Napoleon's defeat. At this point, news of an American victory at Plattsburgh, and the British retreat at Baltimore, had reached negotiators.

In His Own Words

"That which appears to me to be wanting in America is not a General, or General officers and troops, but a naval superiority on the Lakes."

Duke of Wellington, November 9, 1814

The British delegation now changed its demands and wanted to negotiate peace based on the two sides keeping the territories they held at that point. This meant the British could keep forts at Niagara and Mackinac, and most of Maine. The Americans would keep forts Erie and Amherstburg. The Americans did not agree.

Above: The United States won the Battle of Lake Erie in September 1813, leaving it more difficult for the British to supply First Nations warriors living in territories to the northwest of the lake.

Reaching a compromise

The British government asked the Duke of Wellington to take command of the forces in North America. The duke agreed but advised that in order to win the war the British needed a navy better equipped and trained than the Americans on the Great Lakes. Without that, he did not feel the British could protect their territory or gain any territory from the United States. He urged the prime minister to make peace immediately.

The duke's opinion greatly concerned the British prime minister, the Earl of Liverpool. He was getting word that war with America was hurting Great Britain's position in negotiating peace with other nations in Europe. If war broke out in Europe, he did not want the Duke of Wellington and a large number of British troops away in North America.

The British decided to compromise. They dropped their demands for specific lands in North America and both parties agreed to settle based on the way things were before the war. They decided that specific issues, such as the border and fishing rights, were to be decided by commissions afterward.

Above: British prime minister from 1812 to 1827, Robert Banks Jenkinson, Earl of Liverpool, was concerned about reaching settlements from wars against Napoleon and the United States.

Right: Arthur Wellesley, Duke of Wellington, commanded the British forces in Europe and defeated Napoleon. His opinion on how to win the war in North America was highly respected, although he never set foot on the continent.

Signed but not sealed

The final agreement made no reference to one of the causes of the war—the impressment of sailors into British service. Great Britain had stopped this practice anyway with the end of war against Napoleon. Great Britain also dropped its demand for a Native North American territory. It kept its demands for control of islands in Passamaquoddy Bay that lay between the U.S. state of Maine and the British colony of New Brunswick, and for the right to navigate the Mississippi River. It also wanted to take away the U.S. right to fish on land in Newfoundland. The treaty agreed to set these matters aside to be negotiated after the two nations made peace. The Americans agreed to take neither revenge on, or land from, Native North Americans who had been allies of the British.

Below: This engraving shows a monument on the St. Croix River marking the boundary between New Brunswick, Canada, and Maine, United States, as decided at the Treaty of Paris in 1783. After all the fighting, these were the boundaries still used after the War of 1812.

The official end of the war

The treaty was signed on December 24, 1814. However, this did not immediately end the fighting, nor did it end the war. The treaty still needed to be ratified, or agreed to, by each side. The British ratified the agreement on December 27, 1814. It took longer for the Americans to ratify it because it took the U.S. delegates several weeks to travel back to Washington, D.C. As they did so, the Battle of New Orleans took place on January 8, 1815. The Battle of Fort Bowyer in Mobile, Alabama, on February 12, 1815, was the last land action to take place. On February 16, 1815, the U.S. Senate agreed to the treaty and then President Madison ratified it. That officially ended the war.

Below: A public letter by U.S. Secretary of State James Madison, dated January 5, 1804, describes the unlawfulness of impressment. In the end, the Treaty of Ghent made no mention of this issue.

In His Own Words

"The terms of this instrument are undoubtedly not such as our Country expected at the commencement of the War. Judged of however by the actual condition of things … they cannot be pronounced very unfavorable. We lose no territory, I think no honor."

Henry Clay,
December 25, 1814

IMPORTANT

AND

LUMINOUS COMMUNICATION

ON THE

SUBJECT OF THE

IMPRESSMENT OF AMERICAN AND FOREIGN

SEAMEN

AND OTHER PERSONS.

IT has become manifest to every attentive observer, that the early and continued aggressions of Great Britain on our persons, our property, and our rights, imperiously demand a firm stand—an effectual, though calm system of measures of arrestation. For this purpose, it is our duty to make ourselves completely masters of the great truths and arguments by which our rights have been elucidated, supported and maintained. On the 17th of January, 1806, the President of the United States communicated to Congress an extract from a dispatch of James Madison Esq. our secretary of state, to James Monroe Esq. our minister in London, which contains many facts highly important, and observations and arguments perfectly satisfactory and conclusive against "*impressments* of seamen and passengers, whether Foreign or American, on board of our vessels." The republication of that document at this crisis will at once display some of the reasons on which the government has probably declined to sanction the recent draught of a treaty with Great Britain, and will elucidate the ground on which the question of *the impressment of persons*, both native and alien, has been rested by our administration.

Even so, it took some time for the news to reach all areas of the continent and the ships at sea. Sea battles continued until June 30.

The cost of the war

It is estimated that 2,260 Americans were killed in battle and about 15,000 died in total, most as a result of diseases, wounds, and accidents. Estimates on the side of the British say 2,733 soldiers died in battle, with around 10,000 deaths in total. Regarding the number of Native North Americans killed, historians have estimated the total figure to be around 10,000.

War was hard on civilians, too. Property was damaged during the war. Soldiers on both sides of the war used rail fences for firewood and took livestock and produce from farms. Both sides burned government and military property, including the U.S. president's home, and ordinary people's homes and stores. Citizens were robbed and assaulted by soldiers or militiamen. Acts of revenge on prisoners-of-war occurred on both sides. Those living on either bank of the Niagara River were most affected.

Above: James Lawrence, commander of the U.S.S. *Chesapeake* during the famous victory by H.M.S. *Shannon* over the *Chesapeake* on June 1, 1813, was mortally wounded in the battle.

Tying up the loose ends

The outstanding issues that were not dealt with specifically in the Treaty of Ghent were resolved years later and had results that last today.

The boundaries between the United States and British North America were the first to be settled. The first commissions set up in 1816 decided the boundary from the St. Lawrence to the western edge of Lake Superior. The boundary between Lake of the Woods to the Rocky Mountains was set along the 49th parallel by the Convention of 1818.

The boundaries between Maine, New Brunswick, and Lower Canada, as well as the boundary between Lake Superior and Lake of the Woods, were not agreed until the Webster–Ashburton Treaty of 1842. The boundary from the Rocky Mountains to the Pacific Ocean was not set until the Oregon Treaty of 1846, with a dispute over the water boundary settled in 1872. Northern borders with Alaska would be settled later still.

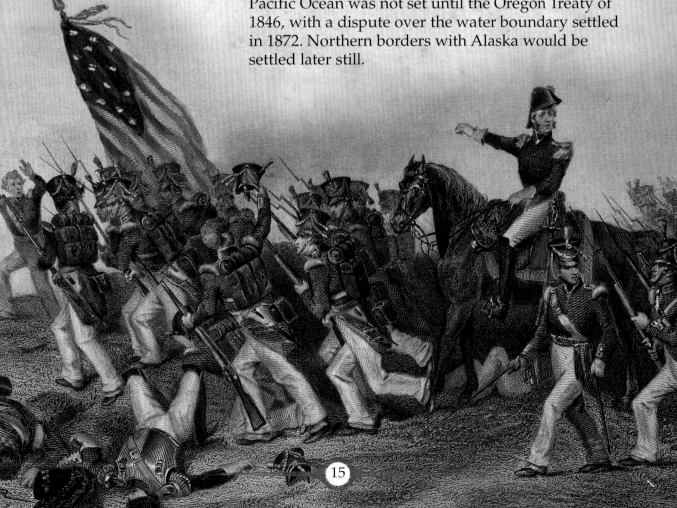

Below: Lieutenant Colonel Winfield Scott ordered the charge of McNeil's battalion at the Battle of Chippawa on July 5, 1814. The U.S. forces defeated a British army of roughly equal size for the first time on an open plain.

Fishing rights

For a time, British ships captured U.S. vessels fishing inside what the British felt were their boundaries. It feared that the United States might retaliate, and Great Britain realized it could not patrol this area without a big fleet of ships and great expense. The United States saw that it would not get everything it wanted without fighting Great Britain. Finally, in 1818, it was decided the Americans could fish along the western and southern coasts of Newfoundland, around the Magdalen Islands, and along the coast of Labrador. They were given the right to enter any bay to find wood and water, to take shelter from a storm, and to repair damage to a ship.

Disarming the Lakes: the Rush–Bagot Agreement

During the war, both the United States and Great Britain competed to build bigger and better ships. Great Britain built two ships in 1814 that would have been more powerful than the British Navy's ocean ships. The United States was building two just as powerful and even larger ships. The Americans proposed that neither side maintain a navy on the Great Lakes and that both keep only enough armed ships to deal with smugglers and criminals.

Above: This photograph shows the U.S.S. *Niagara* during the 1912 centenary of the war.

Below: This photograph shows a detail of the rigging of U.S.S. *Niagara* that has recently been restored.

In April 1817, both sides agreed to the Rush–Bagot Agreement. It was named after the two men who exchanged the letters that spelled out the agreement's terms, Richard Rush, U.S. Acting-Secretary of State, and Charles Bagot, British minister to the United States. The agreement stated each side would keep only one ship each on Lake Ontario and Lake Champlain, and two ships each on the upper lakes. Both sides, however, continued to build forts on land.

Below: Following the war, shipyards along the Atlantic Coast built new vessels to restore the U.S. merchant fleet.

In His Own Words

"The Undersigned, His Britannic Majesty's Envoy Extraordinary and Minister Plenipotentiary, has the honour to acquaint Mr. Rush that having laid before His Majesty's Government the correspondence which passed last year between the Secretary of the Department of State and the Undersigned upon the subject of a proposal to reduce the Naval Force of the respective countries upon the American lakes he has received the commands of His Royal Highness the Prince Regent to acquaint the Government of the United States, that His Royal Highness is willing to accede to the proposition made to the Undersigned by the Secretary of the Department of State in his Note of the 2nd of August last."

Charles Bagot in a letter to Richard Rush

Chapter Two: Nationalism in the U.S.A. and Canada

The American Flag

Before the Battle of Fort McHenry and Francis Scott Key's song, the flag was not such an important national symbol. Flags were flown to identify who was in charge of a fort or a ship. At the time, the official U.S. flag had 15 stripes and 15 stars.

After the war, in 1818, Congress authorized a new flag that had 20 stars—one for each state in the Union—and 13 stripes—one for each of the original 13 former British colonies. It allowed for new stars to be added when a new state joined the Union.

Although the design of the official flag would change in years to come as new states entered the Union, it was Key's song that highlighted the importance of the flag to the United States. The song mentions that in the morning Key was proud to see the flag flying over the fort. Through his song, the flag came to be equated with national pride. The large flag that flew over the fort that morning has been preserved in the Smithsonian Museum.

Although the War of 1812 was inconclusive, it set both Canada and the United States on separate political paths. It also set up a relationship of respect and negotiation between Great Britain, the United States, and later independent Canada.

Changes in the United States

For Americans, a sense of pride arose from their ability to win important victories against the British. Many icons, symbols, and heroes originated from this war. The following are some of the main examples.

Above: A copy of the U.S. flag from 1812 shows 15 stars and 15 stripes.

Right: Francis Scott Key looks at the flag flying over Fort McHenry.

Uncle Sam

In the same way the name John Bull was used to refer to the British government, in 1813 the name Uncle Sam was first used to refer to the U.S. government. The name is said to have come from the initials "U.S.," which were stamped on government shipments of guns, swords, and supplies to the army. It has also been linked to a New York meat packer named Samuel Wilson, whose nickname was Uncle Sam and who supplied the troops with salted beef. The name gradually gained popularity after the war and replaced other representations of the government such as Brother Jonathan by the 1860s.

Manifest Destiny

The United States was free to expand to the West once the British dropped their demand for a Native North American territory. In 1818, Andrew Jackson invaded Spanish-owned Florida, attacking the Seminole Native people for raiding American settlements. Spain decided it would cost too much to defend its territories in North America. By the Adams–Onis Treaty of 1819, Spain gave Florida to the United States and gave up all its lands in the Pacific Northwest. This allowed the United States to claim the West Coast. The term "Manifest Destiny" is used to describe this westward expansion of the United States.

After the war, the United States entered a period known as the "Era of Good Feeling," which lasted from about 1815 to 1825. James

Below: Uncle Sam guards the American continent against European interference in this cartoon of the time. It also illustrates the policy of the U.S. government, known as the Monroe Doctrine, declared in 1823 (see page 20).

Monroe was elected president in 1816 and then re-elected in 1820 with a nearly unanimous vote. In 1823, the Monroe Doctrine became government policy. It announced that the United States would not interfere in matters in Europe and would not accept any European interference in the Americas.

National bank

The need for a national bank soon became evident. In 1816, the Second Bank of the United States was established. It provided currency for businesses and offered loans. In 1819, panic broke out when the economy took a downturn. American products were not in demand so much because, with Europe recovering from the war with Napoleon, Europeans turned to growing their own food and manufacturing their own goods. Many Americans had bought land out west for high prices and could not repay their loans.

Below: In this painting of 1873 the female figure of America leads pioneers and railroads westward. This growth was called the Manifest Destiny, which is the belief that expansion across the continent was inevitable and necessary.

Many land speculators and businesses lost fortunes. But within three years the situation had improved greatly.

Army and navy

It became clear during the war that the army needed to change how it got supplies to its troops and how it trained and organized itself. In addition, militiamen were found to be unreliable because they were not trained, did not always live near the fighting, and their numbers were hard to predict.

The government approved the creation of a standing army so that trained forces would always be ready to defend the country. The army opened up several military schools to train engineers and military officers. Coastal defenses were strengthened as forts were built at major harbors. A system of 200 forts was planned, but only 30 were built between 1816 and 1867. Although the United States would go on to have its own civil war from 1861 to 1865, it had declared to the world that it was now a strong and independent nation.

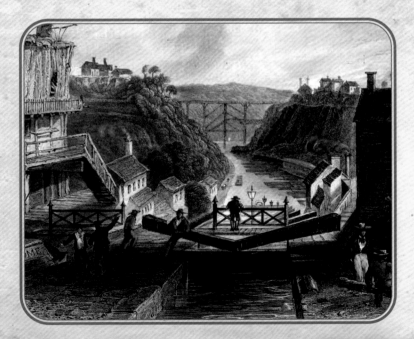

Improved Transportation

Transportation routes in the United States expanded during this period. Paddlewheel steamers moved goods and people along the Mississippi River. In 1817, construction began on the Erie Canal to connect the Hudson River to the Great Lakes. Other canals were built on the Ohio River and its tributaries.

By 1818, the government-funded National Road had been built from Cumberland, Maryland, to Wheeling, Virginia. Other private toll roads added to the new land-based transportation routes. Railroads were constructed beginning in 1828 so that, by 1860, there were some 30,000 miles (48,280 kilometers) of rails in use.

Left: A lock gate on the Erie Canal at Lockport, New York, raised or lowered canal barges so they could continue their journey on the canal.

Canada begins to form an identity

After the War of 1812, Canada remained under British rule. There was less need to add to a national identity with war stories because it was still ruled by Great Britain. These stories did emerge, however, if more slowly than U.S. folklore about the war.

With a smaller population, there were fewer people to study and record the war in detail. It gave Canada a sense of collective achievement against a common enemy. It also helped unite the separate provinces and created a new desire to continue to be governed by a monarchy, and not a republic. Fifty years later, the provinces most effected by the War of 1812 joined together to form the Dominion of Canada. The following pages highlight famous people and national issues related to the war.

The Family Compact

Men who were leaders during the war, such as Bishop John Strachan, William Allan, J. B. Robinson, and Christopher Hagerman, felt they should continue to lead the government of Upper Canada at York after the war. They became known as the Family Compact for their ties to one another. These men promoted their own loyalty to Great Britain during the war and attacked opponents for being disloyal.

Tecumseh and Teyoninhokarawen

The contributions of Native North American warriors were essential in resisting U.S. invasion along the Niagara battlefront. Tecumseh, who fought with General Brock in the victory at Detroit, is remembered as a savior of Canada.

John Norton, a Scottish Cherokee also known as Teyoninhokarawen, was a Mohawk war chief who led Native North Americans in the battles of Queenston Heights, Stoney Creek, Beaver Dams, and others. To recognize his services, he was brevetted to the rank of major in the British Indian Department—that is, he was given the rank and pay but only while employed on active service.

Isaac Brock

British-born Major-General Isaac Brock commanded Canadian forces to victory, with the help of Tecumseh and his warriors, at the surrender of Detroit. He was knighted for this victory, but died on the battlefield at Queenston Heights on October 13, 1812.

Charles-Michel de Salaberry

Colonel Charles-Michel de Salaberry was a British Army officer who was born in Canada. He commanded the Canadian Voltigeurs in the victory at the Battle of Chateauguay. The Voltigeurs were full-time soldiers from Lower Canada.

Laura Secord

Born in Massachusetts, Laura Secord came to Upper Canada in 1795. She overheard American plans to attack at Beaver Dams. On June 22, 1813, she walked almost 20 miles (32 kilometers) to warn the British. Her efforts were not recognized until 1860, when she was 85 years old, but she is one of the most famous Canadian figures from the war.

They wanted Upper Canada to be closely tied to Great Britain and were opposed to U.S. ideals of republican government. Although they were not successful in implementing it, they proposed a state church in Canada, and they did establish a public school system with government financial support.

Compensation

After the war the British government acknowledged that Canadians should be compensated for war-related damages, as much of the war was fought in Upper Canada. However, Great Britain was slow to make payments. It was also difficult to prove who deserved the money. Disagreements arose over feelings that only those in positions of power received compensation while regular citizens were

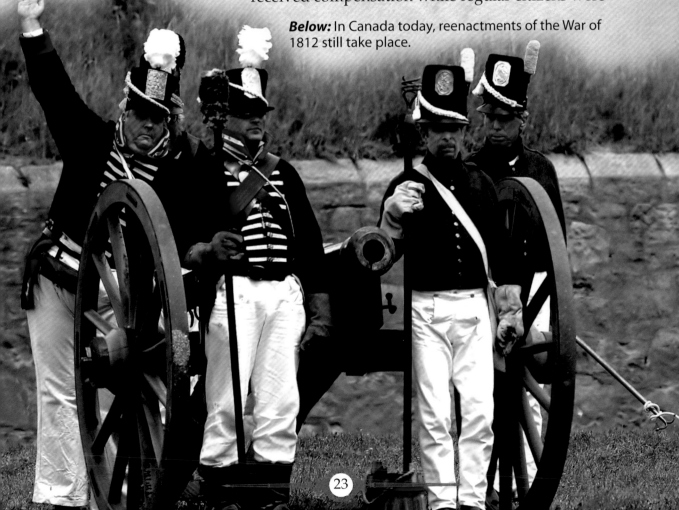

Below: In Canada today, reenactments of the War of 1812 still take place.

The Loyal and Patriotic Society of Upper Canada

This charity was set up in 1814 by Reverend John Strachan to raise money for families of militiamen killed or wounded during the war. It continued until 1817, when the money that had not been used was given to a society that helped poor people. When £4,000 (worth about $6,000 U.S. today) was given to the society from England, it was used to start a hospital in York.

overlooked. In the end, many payments took as long as 20 years to come through and Upper Canada had to contribute to the funds.

American Aliens

The government granted land in Upper Canada to those who were loyal to Great Britain during the war and took away land from those found to have been disloyal. Laws passed on March 14, 1814, meant people thought to have supported the United States could be held for trial and charged with treason. Anyone who had left for the United States after July 1812 was declared an alien and their property was seized by the government.

Below: Some of the buildings and a cannon can be seen at Fort York National Historic Site in Toronto.

Above: This photograph from 1890 shows the monument to Brock at Queenston Heights, Ontario. It stands 184 feet (56 meters) tall.

Left: The statue of Major-General Isaac Brock, as it looks today, stands atop the column.

Monuments and museums

Plans for a monument to commemorate Major-General Isaac Brock and his role in the war were passed in 1814, but it took some time to get the funding together. Construction on the monument began in spring 1823. When it was finished in October 1824, it was the tallest structure in North America at the time. It became such a symbol of Brock's heroism and British power that Benjamin Lett, an Irish-Canadian terrorist with anti-British feelings, destroyed it in 1840. The monument was redesigned and the new version completed in 1856.

Canadians came to realize their history was being swallowed by urban expansion or falling into decay. They took steps to preserve some of the battle sites and forts from the war. Many forts and museums are now National Historic Sites operated by the government agency Parks Canada. They continue to reenact battles and demonstrate the way life was lived during the war. Monuments and historical plaques recording the battles and heroes of the war can be visited today.

Chapter Three: In Search of Land and Freedom

Native North Americans fought on both sides of the war in order to maintain or take back lands they and their ancestors had hunted, fished, and lived on. They fought for the side they felt would ensure that goal. Leaders such as Seneca chief Red Jacket and Shawnee leader Black Hoof fought for the Americans. Those who fought for the British included Shawnee brothers Tecumseh and Tenskwatawa, Scottish-Cherokee John Norton, Mohawk John Brant, Potawatomi leader Main Poc, Sauk leader Black Hawk, and William Weatherford of the Creek nation. The Native North American presence on the battlefield greatly contributed to battles defending Upper Canada, and was critical in capturing forts at Detroit, Mackinac, and Chicago.

Above: A picture painted in the 1870s shows Sauk leader Black Hawk.

Right: A scene from the Battle of the Thames shows the death of Tecumseh by the Kentucky mounted volunteers led by Colonel Richard M. Johnson, October 5, 1813.

Below: American engineer and explorer Major Stephen H. Long meets with members from the Pawnee nation during his expedition to the Rocky Mountains in 1819 to 1820.

Native North Americans suffer on many accounts

First, with Tecumseh's death, his idea for Native people to set aside their differences to fight against the Americans disappeared. Also, the British had dropped their demand for a Native North American territory. Second, Native people suffered as a result of war and diseases introduced by European settlers. Third, Native North Americans that lived in the United States did not receive any military pension from the British even if they were allies. No longer at war, the British did not need them as allies. Also, Native people were no longer needed as economic partners, due to the rise of agriculture and the decline of the fur trade.

Native people everywhere faced the pressure of new settlers moving into their homelands. As they were forced to give up the use of these areas, their traditional ways of living were no longer possible.

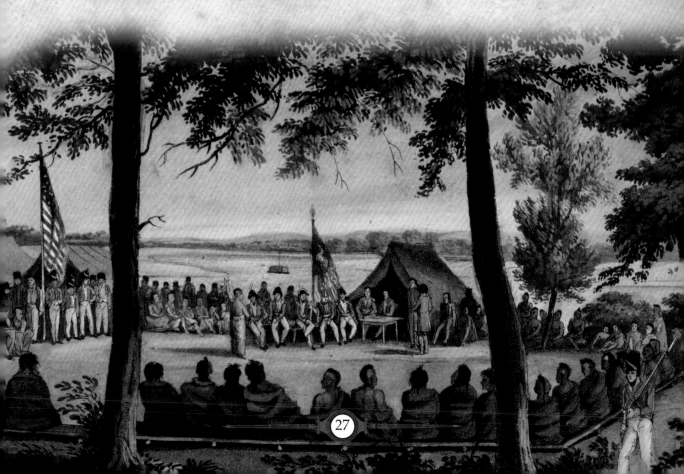

The Indian Removal Act

When the Creek nation was defeated in the southeast United States, and Spain gave territory that was traditional Native land to the U.S. government, expansion into Native homelands could not be stopped. Native people were not able to recover lands they had lost and they could not hold on to the areas they lived in. In the United States they were soon outnumbered by settlers, and they faced similar pressures in Canada.

Settlers poured into the U.S. interior. Native North American treaties were not upheld. When gold was discovered on their lands, the U.S. government arranged to give Native people lands farther west. The Indian Removal Act of 1830 gave the U.S. president power to negotiate with the Native people to give up their lands east of the Mississippi and to move them to areas west of the river. Transportation and compensation costs of $500,000 were set aside, although some nations sold their own lands and relocated. Others fought to stay. By 1837, some 46,000 Native people moved westward either voluntarily or by force. New treaties signed led to the removal of

Above: This painting done in 1942 commemorates the suffering the Cherokee people endured as they were forced to move from their homes in 1838–1839.

Trail of Tears

A Cherokee survivor remembers the Trail of Tears:

"Long time we travel on way to new land. People feel bad when they leave Old Nation. Womens cry and make sad wails. Children cry and many men cry ... but they say nothing and just put heads down and keep on go towards West. Many days pass and people die very much."

even more. In the best-known forced removal, the Trail of Tears, an estimated 16,000 Cherokees were forced to move. An estimated 4,000 died on the journey to Oklahoma from starvation, exposure, or disease.

Setting up reservations

Governments in both the United States and Canada set aside lands for Native people to use. These lands, often called reserves or reservations, were held by the government for use by Native people and the nations would receive money and supplies. Native people were also actively encouraged, and sometimes forced, to convert to Christianity and abandon their own religions and languages. Reserves were often remotely located, making it difficult for Native people to support themselves. Many became dependent on the state for their living.

Below: Chief Crowfoot of the Blackfoot nation in Alberta addresses the Canadian governor- general in 1881 to describe the difficult living conditions and poverty his people were facing.

Below: A photograph from 1891 shows Pine Ridge Indian Reservation in South Dakota.

African Americans fought for both sides

African Americans played an important part in the War of 1812 on both sides. Most African Americans in the United States were slaves, but there were about 200,000 free African Americans in the country at the time. Many served in the U.S. Army militia. About 10 percent of crews on U.S. warships and 20 percent of crews on privateers were African Americans. An even larger proportion of the crew on gunboats were African Americans because few white men volunteered for this dangerous duty.

"They stripped to the waist and fought like devils ... utterly insensible to danger and ... possessed with a determination to outfight the white sailors."

Captain Isaac Hull of the U.S.S. *Constitution*, writing in his official report

Below left: This flyer shows a reward for turning in a runaway slave. Helping a runaway slave had been illegal in the United States since 1793. Slaves were promised freedom if they fought for the British.

$150 REWARD

RANAWAY from the subscriber, on the night of the 2d instant, a negro man, who calls himself *Henry May*, about 22 years old, 5 feet 6 or 8 inches high, ordinary color, rather chunky built, bushy head, and has it divided mostly on one side, and keeps it very nicely combed; has been raised in the house, and is a first rate dining-room servant, and was in a tavern in Louisville for 18 months. I expect he is now in Louisville trying to make his escape to a free state, (in all probability to Cincinnati, Ohio.) Perhaps he may try to get employment on a steamboat. He is a good cook, and is handy in any capacity as a house servant. Had on when he left, a dark cassinett coatee, and dark striped cassinett pantaloons, new—he had other clothing. I will give **$50** reward if taken in Louisvill; **100** dollars if taken one hundred miles from Louisville in this State, and 150 dollars if taken out of this State, and delivered to me, or secured in any jail so that I can get him again.

WILLIAM BURKE.

Bardstown, Ky., *September 3d*, 1838.

The British side also benefitted from the efforts of people of African heritage. Many from British North America, the West Indies, and the United States joined the Royal Navy as seamen. They also worked on privateers, and regiments of men of African descent from the West Indies served in the fighting at New Orleans. In 1814, the British offered all Americans, including slaves, the choice of entering the navy or army, or being sent as free settlers to

Below: A painting of 1893 by Charles T. Webber shows ordinary people helping escaped slaves on their way to freedom in Canada. The secret routes and hideaways they used became known as the Underground Railroad.

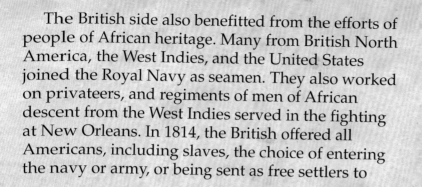

The Story of Harriet Tubman

On the Underground Railroad, people who gave shelter to the slaves were known as stationmasters and guides were called conductors. Harriet Tubman was a slave who, in 1849, escaped from her owner and reached freedom in Pennsylvania. She became a conductor and returned to the South 19 times to lead some 300 escaped slaves to the North. Slave-owners offered a reward for her, but she was never caught.

British colonies in North America or the West Indies. This caused fear of a slave rebellion in the United States. The British set up a base on Tangier Island in Chesapeake Bay, and many slaves fled to this island and the freedom the British offered. Companies of runaways were established in early 1815 as the Corps of Colonial Marines. An estimated 3,601 slaves escaped to freedom in the war.

Colored Corps

In Canada, Richard Pierpoint, a former slave and veteran of the Revolutionary War regiment, Butler's Rangers, asked the government to form a company of militia soldiers of African descent. It did but put a white man, Captain Robert Runchey, in command. Known as Runchey's Company of Colored Volunteers, they fought at the Battle of Queenston Heights. After that battle it was retitled the Colored or Black Corps and reorganized into a militia unit for general service without Runchey, who had died in December 1812. This new unit took part in the Battle of Fort George. Later made part of the Corps of Provincial Military Artificers, the company was sent to repair the fort at the Niagara River and other barracks. The group was disbanded on March 24, 1815. Its members received land grants of 100 acres in new townships set up in Upper Canada. When land grants were given, African Americans received only 100 acres (40 hectares)—half of what white veterans received.

Left: A New York publication of 1847, showing freed slaves against a backdrop of the U.S. Capitol in Washington, D.C., illustrated the growing sense of inhumanity of slavery felt by people in the North.

"That your Excellency's Petitioner is now old and without property that he finds it difficult to obtain a liveliehood by his labour; that he is above all things desirous to return to his native country... and requested aid to return to his African birthplace in exchange for his service with the British army."

Richard Pierpoint,
writing in 1821 to the lieutenant governor

On July 21, 1821, the government wrote of Pierpoint "that he is a faithful and deserving old Negro," but denied him money for the voyage. Pierpoint was instead given 100 acres (40 hectares) of uncleared land. Pierpoint died in poverty about 1838.

Below: A photograph from 1862 shows African-American slaves on a plantation in the Confederate state of South Carolina.

Slavery

In Canada, the first anti-slavery legislation in the British Empire, preventing the importation of enslaved people into Upper Canada and freeing the children of slaves at age 25, was passed in Upper Canada in 1793. Slavery was finally abolished in the British Empire on August 1, 1834.

In the United States, President Lincoln issued the Emancipation Proclamation in September 1862. It stated that unless states rebelling against the Union returned to the Union, the slaves within those states would be declared freed. This tied the issue of slavery to the Civil War of 1861–1865. After the Union Army won the Civil War, the Thirteenth Amendment to the U.S. Constitution was ratified and all slaves were freed in 1865.

Chapter Four: The Aftermath of the War

In His Own Words

Duke of Wellington to Lord Bathurst on December 6, 1825, writing to support the building up of defenses in Canada:

"I entreat your lordship to observe that it is impossible for His Majesty's government to withdraw from these dominions … they must be defended in war."

Below: The Citadel in Quebec is shown here as photographed in 1900.

After the war, Canada and Great Britain felt that the possibility of a U.S. invasion was still a threat. The War of 1812 had shown the weaknesses in Canada's defense system, so work and money was put into building up strategic points and improving transportation routes.

Canals

The trade along the Great Lakes and up the St. Lawrence River had been so important to feed the army during the war. It continued to grow with an expanding population after the war. Food, lumber, fur, and manufactured goods all needed to be moved, but the route was difficult to navigate. Businessmen proposed the building of canals to cut costs and make the route easier to navigate. In 1824 the Lachine Canal opened and the building of the Welland Canal had begun and was finished in 1829.

Three canals on the Ottawa River and the Rideau Canal were built and paid for by the government between 1819 and 1834. This made an alternate route for transporting military supplies between Montreal and Kingston—a route considered essential to Canada's defense.

Fortifications

Although the war was over, Fort Henry continued to be an important defensive structure to guard the entrance to the St. Lawrence River. The war had shown Upper Canada that this was a strategic site to defend. A new fort was built between

1832 and 1837 and it was prepared to defend the St. Lawrence trade and shipping route with troops, guns, and cannons if necessary.

The naval establishment at Penetanguishene was built in 1818 as a base to protect and maintain ships on the upper Great Lakes. It became the base for warships H.M.S. *Tecumseth* and H.M.S. *Newash*. Supply ships moved cargo and supplies and, by 1820, about 20 ships were maintained there. Work on La Citadel in Quebec City began in 1820 because the British felt this spot was also likely to be a target for a U.S. invasion. To the east, the Halifax Citadel was built to guard against a land-based attack from the United States.

Below: Fort Henry, in Kingston, Ontario, is a designated National Historic Site demonstrating and educating people about its history. It was an active fort until 1891.

Immigration

Another way for the British government to help defend Canada was to settle it with loyal citizens. The British government did not encourage Americans to come to Upper Canada because of fears they would be disloyal. Instead, it encouraged settlement mainly by people from Great Britain. Members of the British forces were disbanded and given land. About 600,000 people from England, Scotland, and Ireland emigrated to Canada between 1815 and 1841.

As immigrants poured in, they brought with them an epidemic of cholera and later typhus. These deadly diseases caused panic in Canada, so several quarantine stations were set up. Those who looked sick had to stay on Grosse Île, an island in the middle of the St. Lawrence River, until they either got well or died. Sometimes whole ships of immigrants were quarantined for days before being allowed into port. Thousands of immigrants, mostly from Ireland, died because methods to treat the diseases were not understood at the time.

Right: Reenactors provide information to tourists at Grosse Île in Quebec, which was a quarantine station from 1832 to 1937.

Rebellions

Dissatisfaction with the government after the war led to rebellions in both Upper and Lower Canada in 1837 and 1838. The majority of those elected to government wanted to make changes so that more decisions were made by the elected representatives. But they could not make these changes because the ruling minority—called the Family Compact in Upper Canada and the Chateau Clique in Lower Canada—would not allow it. A minority of the reformers had more radical demands and wanted a U.S.-style, republican form of government with no ties to Britain. These radicals tried to take the government by force but were stopped by British troops and loyal volunteers.

Below: Irish people at the port of Cork pay and wait for their sea passage to Canada. This colored engraving of immigrants was made in 1851.

The aftermath in Great Britain

In Great Britain, the War of 1812 was mostly seen as a small part of the larger war against Napoleon. Shortly after the Treaty of Ghent was ratified, Napoleon returned from exile and once again war with France occupied much of Europe. Great Britain sent the Duke of Wellington—who had not been sent to command the defense of Canada—and an army to fight Napoleon. In a final battle at Waterloo, on June 18, 1815, Napoleon was defeated. Historians speculate that this outcome might have been different had the duke and a large number of troops been sent to Canada.

Once the war in North America was over, many troops returned home to Great Britain. However, the British government offered its war veterans land in Upper Canada in the hope of increasing the local population with those loyal to the country.

Great Britain wanted to keep its land and involvement in North America and it continued to govern Canada. It invested a lot of money in

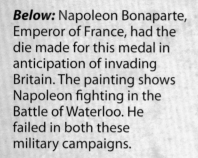

Below: Napoleon Bonaparte, Emperor of France, had the die made for this medal in anticipation of invading Britain. The painting shows Napoleon fighting in the Battle of Waterloo. He failed in both these military campaigns.

building the new citadels, canals, and defense systems in different areas of British North America. Great Britain also renewed trade with the United States and opened its ports in the West Indies to American ships and trade. In 1854, Great Britain negotiated a Reciprocity Treaty with the United States that established free trade between the two countries and with all of British North America.

Confederation for Canada

Upper Canada and Lower Canada joined together in 1841 as the Province of Canada. The colonies of New Brunswick and Nova Scotia joined with them as the Dominion of Canada on Confederation Day, July 1, 1867. The remaining colonies joined in the years that followed, until Canada's borders matched the United States in spanning the North American continent from the Atlantic to the Pacific coast.

Great Britain supported and encouraged the confederation. Yet there were special interest groups that wanted to liberate Canada from British rule. Their goal was to provoke Great Britain to go to war with the United States again. One of these groups, the Fenians, wanted to free Ireland from British rule and saw attacking Canada as a start. Many were Irish veterans of the American Civil War (1861–1865). These groups burned a steamship and fought several battles in 1866–1871.

These attacks were stopped by British and Canadian troops. The aggressive acts helped convince the Maritime Provinces to join Canada in confederation so that by the early 1880s the country was a unified nation.

Below: Canadian flags fly from the top and in front of the tower of the present-day Parliament building in Ottawa.

Left: The Ambassador Bridge spans the Detroit River to connect Detroit, Michigan, with Windsor, Ontario. It is the busiest border crossing between Canada and the United States.

Border, Lakes, and Trade

The border between Canada and the United States is 5,524 miles (8,890 kilometers) long.

The Great Lakes—Superior, Huron, Michigan, Erie, and Ontario—are the largest group of freshwater lakes in the world. They are shared between Canada and the United States. Only Lake Michigan is entirely within the United States. The surface area of all the Great Lakes is 94,595 square miles (245,000 square kilometers).

In 2010, over $1 billion worth of goods and services crossed the border between Canada and the United States every day.

Conclusion

So what were and still are the main legacies of the War of 1812? Canada was not taken over by the United States and kept its ties to Great Britain. That set it on the course for eventually becoming a nation within the British Commonwealth. Great Britain maintained its North American colonies and still won the war with Napoleon. The United States felt that it had successfully proven that its republican form of government worked, and had asserted itself as an independent nation on the world stage.

The relationship between the United States, Great Britain, and Canada has been rocky at times. But after the War of 1812, the nations have managed to solve their differences through diplomacy and negotiation. The nations have often been allies in war and have often been on the same side of international conflicts. Canada and the United States cooperated in building the St. Lawrence International Seaway, expanding and modernizing the route for today's large ships. It was completed in 1959 and gives the interior of all of North America access to trade with the world. The War of 1812 played a key role in shaping the relationships and political geography of North America today.

Remembering the war today

Many sites across the United States and Canada commemorate the war. Museums contain artifacts from the battles; plaques or monuments mark sites of importance; and some forts demonstrate the lifestyle of officers or militiamen and hold special days to reenact the major battles from the war.

In the United States, Old Fort Niagara, Fort McHenry, Fort Meigs, the Battle of Tippecanoe, Battle of New Orleans, Battle of Plattsburg, the U.S.S. *Constitution*, and Sackets Harbor are some of the major sites.

In Canada, Fort Erie, Fort St. Joseph, Fort George, Fort York, the Battle of Chateauguay, and the Battle of Crysler's Farm are some of the sites of interest.

In Great Britain, the Royal Naval Museum and the National Army Museum provide details about the British military. In this way, the memory of the war is preserved so we can understand more about how it helped to shape three great nations of today.

Below: Government leaders from the United States, Canada, Great Britain, and other nations continue to discuss matters of worldwide importance at formal meetings such as the G8 Summit held in Huntsville, Ontario, Canada, in 2010.

GLOSSARY

allies Countries or nations that cooperate with one another to fight on the same side during war

American Civil War The war between the Union states of the North and the Confederacy of the South, fought between 1861 and 1865

American Revolutionary War The war between Great Britain and its 13 American colonies from 1775 to 1783

barracks A building an army uses for its soldiers to live in

border Dividing line or boundary between two countries

civilians People not directly involved in the military or a war

civil war War within a country or between people of the same country

colony A place where people live far from the country that rules it

commissions A group of people responsible for accomplishing a specific goal

Commonwealth A group of independent nations, all of which were once British colonies. The British monarch is the head of the Commonwealth

compensation Money paid to make up for a loss of income, work or property, or for an injury or death

confederation The permanent joining of regions, with most governing power held by a central authority

Congress In the United States, two groups of representatives who make laws for the nation—the Senate and the House of Representatives

constitution System of government, laws, and principles under which a country is governed, often written down in a single document

continent Large landmass containing many countries and regions

defensive Trying to defend or protect yourself or your group

delegates People responsible for representing others at a meeting

deserter Someone who runs away

diplomacy Managing relationships between nations in a peaceful manner using negotiations

epidemic A contagious disease that infects a lot of people over a wide area

Fenians Irish revolutionary group in the United States that sought the independence of Ireland from British rule

folklore Legends, myths, and stories that are traditional of a culture

fortification A building, such as a castle or fort, strengthened to withstand enemy attack

free trade Trade between nations without interference from government such as tariffs

governor-general The king's or queen's representative in a country within the British Commonwealth

Great Lakes The five vast freshwater lakes—Superior, Huron, Michigan, Erie, and Ontario—that lie between Canada and the United States in the center of the continent

gunboat A small ship equipped with guns and used along a coast or river

immigrants People who arrive in a country to live there permanently

impressment The act of forcing someone to be in the navy or army

lieutenant governor The head of a province or colony appointed by the governor-general

Loyalist An American who stayed loyal or friendly to Great Britain

Maritime Provinces The Canadian provinces of New Brunswick, Nova Scotia, and Prince Edward Island that lie next to the Atlantic Ocean

militia Men fighting in a battle who are regular citizens and not full-time members of the army or navy

Napoleonic Wars A series of conflicts between France (led by Napoleon) and other European countries that lasted from 1803 to 1815

national anthem A song of loyalty to one's country

Native North American An inhabitant of North America before the continent was settled by Europeans. Also known as First Nations in Canada

negotiations Meetings and discussions between two or more opposing sides with the goal of coming to an agreement

New England The six states—Maine, Connecticut, Massachusetts, New Hampshire, Rhode Island, and Vermont—that lie in the northeast United States, probably so named because of their likeness to England

parallel Imaginary line that runs around the world east to west to measure latitude

political party A group that is organized to promote certain policies and leaders in government

port A town or city by the water where ships load and unload goods

president The elected head of the U.S. government

prime minister The head of the elected government in Britain; the king's highest representative

privateer A ship owned by a merchant that is given permission by the government to fight in war

quarantine Keeping people suspected of having a contagious disease separate from the general population

ratify To formally approve and agree to something

rebellion An armed uprising against a government

reenactment To act out a past event as accurately as possible

representative Someone who acts or speaks for people as laws are made

republican A form of government in a republic, which is a state where power is held by people and their elected representatives, with an elected president

slavery A system where a person owns another person and makes them do work for no pay

treaty A formal agreement between two parties

veteran A former soldier, sailor, or other person who has fought in a war

War Hawk A person elected to the U.S. Congress, especially from Kentucky, Ohio, and Tennessee, who wanted to go to war against Great Britain

CHRONOLOGY

1814

August 8 Peace talks begin in Ghent in present-day Belgium

August 14 Battle of Fort Erie

August 24–25 Washington burned by British

September 14 Francis Scott Key writes "Star-Spangled Banner"

September 15 Congress of Vienna begins in Austria for European nations to negotiate a peace settlement following the war against Napoleon

December 24 Treaty of Ghent signed

December 27 Great Britain ratifies Treaty of Ghent

1815

January 8 Battle of New Orleans

February 12 Siege at Fort Bowyer, Alabama

February 16 United States ratifies Treaty of Ghent

February 20 U.S. frigate *Constitution* defeats H.M.S. *Cyane* and H.M.S. *Levant*

February 24 Battle of St Mary's River, Georgia

March 16 H.M.S. *Erebus* shoots at U.S. gunboat 168 off coast of Georgia

March 23 U.S. sloop *Hornet* defeats H.M.S. *Penguin* in the South Atlantic

May 24 Battle of Sinkhole, Missouri

June 30 U.S. sloop *Peacock* fights East India cruiser *Nautilu*s in the Indian Ocean near Sumatra

1816–1820

1816 Second Bank of the United States established

1817 Construction of the Erie Canal begins

1817 Rush–Bagot Agreement disarms the Great Lakes

1818 New design for the American flag agreed

1819 Adams–Onis Treaty: Spain gives land in Florida and Pacific Northwest to the United States

1821–1840

1823 Monroe Doctrine declared

1830 Indian Removal Act

1834 Slavery abolished in the British Empire

1837, 1838 Rebellions against the governments of Upper and Lower Canada

1841–1867

1841 Upper Canada and Lower Canada form the Province of Canada

1857 Ottawa is chosen to be the capital of Canada

1861–1865 U.S. Civil War

1865 Thirteenth Amendment to the U.S. Constitution frees American slaves

1867 New Brunswick and Nova Scotia join the Province of Canada to form the confederation of the independent Dominion of Canada

MORE INFORMATION

Greenblatt, Miriam. *The War of 1812*. New York: Facts On File, Inc., 2003.

O'Neill, Robert and Carl Benn. *The War of 1812: The Fight for American Trade Rights*. New York: Rosen Publishing Group, Inc., 2011.

Raatma, Lucia. *The War of 1812*. Minneapolis: Compass Point Books, 2005.

Santella, Andrew. *Cornerstones of Freedom: The War of 1812*. Connecticut: Children's Press, 2001.

Sonneborn, Liz. *The War of 1812*. New York: Rosen Publishing Group, Inc., 2004.

Zimmerman, Dwight Jon. *Tecumseh: Shooting Star of the Shawnee*. New York: Sterling, 2010.

WEBSITES

PBS: The War of 1812
http://www.pbs.org/war-of-1812/index.html

The War of 1812
http://www.warof1812.ca/

The Official War of 1812 Bicentennial
http://www.visit1812.com/history/

1812 History: Canadian Heritage
http://www.1812history.com/

Archives of Ontario: The War of 1812
http://www.archives.gov.on.ca/english/educational-resources/pdf/war-of-1812.pdf

National Archives: Transcript of the Treaty of Ghent
http://www.ourdocuments.gov/doc.php?flash=true&doc=20&page=transcript

St. Lawrence War of 1812 Bicentennial Alliance
http://www.celebrate1812.com/

Archives of Ontario: Soldiering in Canada 1812–1814
http://www.archives.gov.on.ca/english/on-line-exhibits/1812/soldier-life.aspx

The Price of Freedom: America at War, War of 1812, Smithsonian
http://americanhistory.si.edu/militaryhistory/exhibition/flash.html

Trail of Tears, National Historic Trail
http://www.nps.gov/trte/index.htm

BIBLIOGRAPHY

Books

Berton, Pierre. *The Invasion of Canada: 1812–1813*. Toronto: McClelland and Stewart, 1980.

Dale, Ronald J. *The Invasion of Canada: Battles of the War of 1812*. Toronto: James Lorimer & Company Ltd., 2001.

Hickey, Donald R., *Don't Give Up the Ship!: Myths of the War of 1812*. Toronto: Robin Brass Studio, 2006.

Turner, Wesley B. *War of 1812: The War for Canada*. Focus on Canadian History Series. Toronto: Grolier Limited, 1982.

Zuehlke, Mark. *For Honour's Sake: The War of 1812 and the Brokering of an Uneasy Peace*. Alfred A. Knopf, 2006.

DVD

1812: The Forgotten War. DVD. Oakville, ON: Little Brick Schoolhouse, Inc., 1995.

Websites

The War of 1812 website: http://www.warof1812.ca/

The Canadian Encyclopedia: "War of 1812"
http://www.thecanadianencyclopedia.com/index.cfm?PgNm=TCE&Params=a1ARTA0008442

From Colony to Country: A Reader's Guide to Canadian Military History. Collections Canada
http://www.collectionscanada.gc.ca/military/index-e.html

Hickey, Don. *Leading Myths of the War of 1812*. War of 1812, September 2006
http://www.napoleon-series.org/military/Warof1812/2006/Issue4/c_myths.html

War of 1812 magazine: http://www.napoleon-series.org/index.html

Treaty of Ghent
http://www.thecanadianencyclopedia.com/index.cfm?PgNm=TCE&Params=A1ARTA0003243

History of the War of 1812: The Official War of 1812 Bicentennial web site, June 2, 2011
http://www.visit1812.com/history/

Stacey, C.P. *The Undefended Border, the Myth and the Reality*. Ottawa: Canadian Historical Association, 1954.
http://www.collectionscanada.gc.ca/obj/008004/f2/H-1_en.pdf

Aboriginal People in the Canadian Military: Chapter Four, "Transforming Relationships," 1815–1902. http://www.cmp-cpm.forces.gc.ca/dhh-dhp/pub/boo-bro/abo-aut/chapter-chapitre-04-eng.asp

Grosse Île and the Irish Memorial National Historic Site
http://www.pc.gc.ca/lhn-nhs/qc/grosseile/index.aspx

Black History Canada: War of 1812
http://www.blackhistorycanada.ca/events.php?themeid=21&id=5
http://www.nps.gov/fopu/historyculture/the-third-system.htm

Statistics Canada. Censuses of Canada 1665 to 1871
http://www.statcan.gc.ca/pub/98-187-x/4064809-eng.htm

INDEX